70

Golf with Tony Jacklin

Golf with Tony Jacklin

Step by step, a great professional
shows an enthusiastic amateur
how to play every stroke of the game

Michael Barratt

Arthur Barker Limited   London
A subsidiary of Weidenfeld (Publishers) Limited

Published in Great Britain by
Arthur Barker Limited
94 Clapham High Street   London sw4

ISBN 0 213 16684 4

Printed in Great Britain by
Butler & Tanner Ltd, Frome and London

Contents

Introduction

Once upon a time, in the days when I was joint President (with Michael Parkinson) of the Anti-Golf Society, I rashly accepted an invitation to take a stroll round the beautiful tree-lined fairways of the Berkshire Golf Club near Ascot. It was a glorious August afternoon, the kind that confirms an enthusiastic globetrotter in the view that green and pleasant England under an English sky cannot be equalled by any other spot on earth.

My friend Adam, who had invited me to walk with him, made a vain attempt to persuade me to 'take a few clubs and hit a ball about a bit'.

'Let's get this straight from the start,' I told him. 'There is no way you will ever get me to play this daft game. I have better things to do than waste my time hitting a silly little white ball around a golf course hour after hour.'

So I walked while he played ... until we were halfway down the fairway on the seventeenth when Adam took a ball out of his bag, dropped it on the ground, handed me a number five iron and said: 'Have a go.'

'Now look here, Adam, I've already told you that you're wasting your time trying to inveigle me into this ridiculous sport. I've enjoyed your company, the scenery is breathtaking and the walk has no doubt done me good. But I will not spoil it all by attempting to play.'

'Stop blethering and just take a swing at that ball,' said Adam.

Whereupon I did. And there followed the most extraordinary train of developments.

For a start, club face connected with ball so sweetly and rhythmically that I swear my muscles rippled with delight as the ball sailed through the summer air, describing a perfect arc and landing snugly close to the flag.

I have never hit a ball so well since that first careless swing, but any rabbit of a golfer will know the intense pleasure it provided – and will understand what compelled me, on the eighteenth tee, to borrow a wood for a practice drive. I just touched the ball with the toe of the club and fell over in the process, but no matter. I was an instant addict.

I handed in my seals of office to Parky after that (a step which he was to repeat some years later) and bought my first set of second-hand clubs for £20.

A week or two afterwards, having completed my first full round of eighteen holes with some long-suffering friends, I walked off the last green, glanced for the first time that afternoon at my watch – and realized with some astonishment that for the first time in my life I had occupied nearly four hours without once thinking of my programme (I was then fronting 'Nationwide' nightly on television) or of domestic problems. Add to that kind of mental relaxation the bonus of healthy physical exercise and the reasons for my taking up the game were growing.

Soon, too, I learned to appreciate the advantages of golf to nomads like myself working odd hours, often in strange places. When I have an hour or two to spare, I can walk into practically any golf club anywhere and find a partner to play nine or eighteen holes. And because of the handicap system, we'll be well matched however good or bad our individual standards might be. (Let me confess at this point that I'm a twenty-three handicap man myself, which is just about as bad as it's possible to be, yet many's the time I have played a full round with a complete stranger of much greater skill and have remained in contention right up to the last hole.)

I know no other game of which that could be said. There's no point at all trying to play tennis, for instance, against someone who's very much better than you. It's simply no contest. As for cricket, you need to round up twenty-one other players plus a couple of umpires and a scorer before you can even contemplate a game!

For me, golf was quickly to offer much more besides, because I was soon roped into the Pro-Am circuit, which means that I sometimes found myself playing in front of huge crowds to raise money for several charities through societies like the Lord's Taverners, Variety Club and SPARKS (sportsmen pledged to aid research into crippling diseases). The terrors of standing – or rather, quivering – on the first tee, waiting to drive off in front of several thousand people, are too awful to relate here but there has been the enormous satisfaction of earning hundreds of thousands of pounds over the years for the disabled or deprived and at the same time building golfing friendships with some of the great-hearted regulars in these competitions like Henry Cooper, Dickie Henderson, Harry Secombe, Eric Sykes, Jimmy Hill, Colin Cowdrey, Bruce Forsyth, Kevin Keegan and so many more. (Arden Camm, secretary of the SPARKS events, says that he likes me to play in his tournaments because 'you don't mind making a fool of yourself in front of a big crowd'. That will give you a further impression of my golfing skills.)

Now I have long since come to terms with the fact that I'll never be a very good golfer. I started too late in life, with sinews already set in their ways; I can't find the time to practise and play several times a week, and I suspect that something called 'natural aptitude' is in rather short supply, too. But I can, patently, learn how to play much better than I do now, which means – and this has become my prime purpose – that I can learn to *enjoy* my golf a great deal more.

Doesn't that apply to you, too?

The learning process began for me in a state of confusion from which I never properly recovered. I was given an initial hour's lesson by a club professional who introduced me to that haunting word, 'swing', and concentrated in particular on making me swing 'through the ball' (yes, you've heard it all before!).

He then told me: 'I don't want you starting off by trying to swing the club the whole way like a Jacklin or a Nicklaus. That will come in time. I want you to concentrate instead on the bottom half of the circle and for a couple of months at least I don't want to see your club raised in the backswing higher than your elbow.'

He also showed me how to grip a club, with fingers interlocking round the shaft – extremely uncomfortable, of course, but a good grip always is at first.

A couple of days later I came upon the late Tom Haliburton, an old friend from my sports reporting days on a newspaper in Glasgow. He was in the Wentworth clubhouse, where he was the pro, and I told him that at last I'd been enticed into playing golf.

'Great! Let's have a look at you then,' said the big gentle man, leading me round to the practice ground.

I gripped the club and prepared to swing – or swipe.

'Wait a minute,' said Tom. 'What sort of grip do you call that? It can't

9

possibly be comfortable. Take your hands off the club. Now, simply bring them together and grip in the natural way.... That's more like it. Let's see your swing.'

Carefully I brought the club head back, making sure it wasn't more than elbow height.

'Goodness me, what are you doing?' asked the incredulous Tom. 'Let's see a proper swing – right back – go on – I want you to describe a full circle.'

As I say, I was hopelessly confused by the conflicting advice from two professional teachers. What was I supposed to do? Whose advice should I follow?

In the event, I took the arrogant way out by deciding to 'do it my way', eschewing lessons and somehow believing that if I hit balls hard enough and often enough I'd develop a technique of my own. Apart from the fact that such an approach to the game was extraordinarily stupid, my confusion was confounded by all my new-found golfing friends who, from the exalted positions of fifteen or sixteen handicaps, all knew precisely what was wrong with my game. My backswing was too fast; I was coming across the ball; my stance was too open; my stance was too closed; I had the wrong grip; I was lifting my head, failing to follow through – and all the rest of a golfing rabbit's compendium of errors.

I was later privileged to be given lessons by some of the world's golfing greats. At Troon before a British Open championship, Arnold Palmer took me in hand. He did his best to stop me swaying and slicing but in the end asked me ever so pleasantly:

'Do you really think it's a good idea to play golf?'

On the eve of another Open, at Lytham St Annes, Gary Player tried to teach me how to improve my swing with a smooth and full follow-through, something he reckoned was a prime ingredient of success. Finally, when words failed him, he took out a club and gave me an impression of how I was hitting the ball. It looked for all the world like the shot of a misshapen contortionist.

Unwittingly, however, Arnold and Gary had given me what I like to think is a bright idea, one that is the basis for the book you're reading now.

Their lessons were transmitted on the 'Nationwide' programme, which meant that up to eleven million people were able to laugh at my discomfiture, but it also meant that some of the things that were wrong with my golf became glaringly obvious to me when the transmissions were recorded and later played back to me. To be able to see the way I struck a ball in contrast to Arnold or Gary suddenly brought home to me all the things they and others had unavailingly been trying to tell me for so long.

Put it another way: Look at a picture in a book of, say, Jack Nicklaus driving, or watch him on film. You'll be thrilled by the rhythm of his action and long to emulate it, though you may think to yourself: 'That's the way I execute a drive when I'm standing on the tee. So why don't I hit the ball straight and true like him?'

Now imagine you could watch a poor amateur golfer (or even yourself) playing beside Nicklaus. Wouldn't that bring out the differences as no words or diagrams could do?

With this principle in mind, I've set out to produce an entertaining golfing lesson in book form which contrasts my own execrable (but perhaps not uncommon) style with that of the greatest British golfer since the war.

I confess to choosing Tony Jacklin as my teacher in part because I enjoy his friendship. But putting that consideration aside, solid achievement makes him the Briton we'd all most want to learn from. Ignoring the flashy claims for new stars who come and go with ultrasonic speed in the British golfing firmament, there is no disputing Tony's place at the top. Let me remind you of some of his tournament successes.

After graduating from the American qualifying school in 1967, he joined the Tour and promptly won the Jacksonville Open with a record 15-under-par 273. And then he took the jackpot. He won the British Open in 1969 and soon after that the US Open – a historic double because he became the only British player in the history of the game to have held both titles at the same time. A whole string of American and European championship wins have followed.

However, statistics do not tell all. A remarkable element in the Jacklin story is his emergence as an outstanding teacher – a talent by no means possessed by all top golfers. In the last year or two there has been a growing demand for Jacklin 'clinics' at British clubs as word has spread of Tony's special knack of improving the amateur's game.

My own lesson, admittedly a privileged one, took the form of a nine-hole match we played together on the La Moye course in Jersey, where Tony has made his home since 1975. It was, let us confess, a rather chauvinistic outing. As Tony and I strode down the fairways we were followed by his wife Vivien struggling along behind carrying his clubs – and my

The sound recordist, my
wife Dilys, and the caddie,
Tony's wife Vivien, make
up the four on Jersey's La
Moye course.

wife Dilys panting beside us with a heavy tape recorder so that our conversation, and in particular Tony's on-the-spot advice, could be transcribed in the following pages.

After playing, and learning from the real situations that most of us come up against in a round of golf, we retired to Tony's home for a more relaxed discussion (reported in 'The Home Half' chapter) on fundamentals. Later still we followed the Jacklins to Phoenix, Arizona, to complete our education by seeing how his clubs are made – and thereby learning a thing or two about how to choose clubs for our more modest purposes.

One more thing. As a result of putting this book together by actually *playing* with Tony Jacklin, my own game has improved unbelievably and so in consequence has my enjoyment of it.

If you can say the same after reading the book and putting Tony's advice into practice, we'll have holed in one!

The First

par 4, 365 yards

Off the tee with a wood

The backswing of Tony ...

and the half-back (or half-baked) swing of mine.

The end of Tony's swing, the full follow-through ... and my swing?

It's the end! 'You didn't swing with your arms,' he tells me.

I stand on the first tee blushing with the remembrance of the last time I was here, playing in a Variety Club Cel-Am tournament and making an absolute ass of myself. It was probably the worst round I've ever played in my life, and that's saying something. We played then in rain that came down in stair rods. Today the skies are grey and there's a cold wind blowing.

I take my number one wood and drive the ball in a spinning curve to the left of the fairway, and into the light rough, about 160 yards away. Tony laughs, which is the reaction I usually get to my tee shots, but concedes that for me it wasn't bad. But what was wrong?

TONY The tendency is for your hands to be spread apart. That means they don't work together; they're working against one another. The important objective is to use both hands as one – whether it's with the overlapping grip, the interlocking grip or the two-fisted grip, which you use, which means that all the fingers of both your hands are on the club. But you must keep your hands together.

Your grip's fine in the sense that the Vs between the index finger and thumb of both hands point on a line between the chin and opposite shoulder. But you have your hands spread apart so that they're working against each other.

If I was actually recommending a grip to you, I would suggest that you overlap the little finger of your right hand on top of the forefinger of your left. However, you can choose the grip that suits you best provided always that both hands are working in unison.

The reason that my grip is 'correct' and yours is questionable is the fact that my hands are both in a neutral position. I'm not struggling to force the club in different directions. And therefore I'm more liable to be able to take the club away from the ball consistently, all the time.

You have small hands and although they're strong, they have short fat fingers, which makes me think you ought to try the interlocking grip with the little finger of your right hand locked into the forefinger of your left. A fellow called Jack Nicklaus does that and it hasn't done him any harm!

Now you're getting confused because I've given you reasons for using any of the grips! What you must do is find the one that brings the best results for you. It's a personal thing, but whichever grip you finally settle on, there is one unbreakable rule – that you must use both hands together as a single unit.

MIKE Well, I'm trying the overlapping grip but it hurts my hands. It's really uncomfortable.

TONY Nevertheless, I suggest you should persevere. You're obviously attracted to the sort of advice that some people give, to make yourself comfortable within certain bounds. But I don't agree with that because it usually means that you alter the grip a little more and a little more ... until you're so comfortable that you've got it all wrong!

Get the grip right and you'd be amazed how, after persisting with it for one full round without letting the hands slip into sloppy ways, the grip becomes natural to you.

We reach my ball on the left of the fairway with a slight rise in the ground in front. Tony advises a seven iron to give the ball enough lift and, painfully using my more 'together' grip, I hit a pretty good shot – into more rough, it's true, but quite close to the green. Meanwhile Tony's ball, from his drive, is on an upward slope and also in semi-rough.

MIKE Now that would be a very difficult shot for me because it's on a slope and I've never understood how to address a ball in a position like that.

21

Hands apart – right and wrong.

Reverse view of the two-fisted grip. The hands indicate that there is less chance of their working together than in . . .

the overlapping – or Vardon – grip of Tony's. This position encourages a 'one-piece' movement.

The grip

Mike changes to the
overlapping grip.

Close-up of Tony's
overlapping grip from the
other angle.

Keeping balance

Off an upward lie, Tony shows how he has compromised his stance in order to feel comfortable, realizing that the lie will cause the ball to move right to left because of the weight distribution.

TONY In a situation like this with an awkward stance, an awkward lie, I must first keep my balance. That's the most important thing. So it's essential not to be taking a club that I've got to lash at very hard. I'm taking a nine iron. The distance to the flag is about 110 yards, so I'm playing well within myself and not trying any heroics. Just a gentle swing through the ball ...

He's on the green.

MIKE You make it look so easy, but I'm still not sure what the basic rules are for hitting balls off sloping lies.

TONY Off an upward lie, it's very difficult to maintain your weight forward and the tendency is for the ball to hook, or draw, off such a lie. Therefore I aim fractionally right of target, allowing for that hook to happen quite naturally.

For the downward lie, again the important thing is to 'stay down' on the ball (otherwise you top it) and aim to the left. It's impossible on a down slope for you to keep going 'through' the ball for very long. You'd come up from it quite quickly and the ball would tend to spin off a little to the right, so in this case you want to aim slightly to the left to compensate for that.

From my position in rough grass close to the green, I study my third shot as Tony gives me advice.

TONY You've got to make your mind up here about just two things. You've got to lift the ball well enough to get it out of the long grass – and you must also imagine how the ball's going to react when it's out. The thing that you don't want to do is to lob it too high from here. There's no necessity to do that. So in a situation like this you want to be taking something like a seven or a six iron, and just *feeling* the distance of it, as you would a putt. Essentially it's much the same shot as a putt but the loft on the club will just elevate it enough to ...

Impatiently I have a stab at the ball before he's finished talking. It bounces to the edge of the green, yards short.

The sloping lie

Tony demonstrates how to tackle a sloping lie. Balance is the essential. Here, on an upward slope, he aims slightly right of the flag, allowing for the ball to hook (or curve to the left) quite naturally.

In the rough, close to the green, Tony explains about 'feeling' the distance.

'One smooth swing action ...
look at the hole, and your eye and mind tell you the rest.'

My stance is all wrong (the comparison with Tony's tells it all)
... and I am about to stab at the ball instead of swinging through it.

TONY The back swing was a little bit long and you had to decelerate. You were going to strike too hard and you sort of decelerated just before striking the ball, rather than keeping it all in one smooth swinging action. As I said – though you were in too much of a hurry to listen properly – you *feel* it. Look, how would I get the right distance if I was throwing a ball with my hand to that pole? I can't tell you any more than that. I would throw it and my eye would tell me how hard to do so. The same with this ball. You look at the hole, and your eye and mind tell you the rest.

I putt and miss. Tony holes his and I'm one down, despite my handicap advantage of a shot a hole.

MIKE I wish you'd explain how I'm supposed to 'read' a green. I watch the experts getting down on their knees and having a look, but I'm never quite sure what they're looking for.

TONY Essentially you look for undulations, to tell you which way the land falls. The other thing you're looking for is the way the grass grows – not so important in Britain because our grasses are of a soft texture, but vital in places like Africa and South America where they grow different, coarser grasses. If it's going to slow the ball down, or if there's any particular very grassy or fluffy patch near the hole that you think might slow the ball down a bit, you give it a bit extra.

The majority of professionals, when they walk on to a green, have a pretty well-established idea in their minds on what line to hit the ball, just from the way that the green 'sits'. The shenanigans on the green, walking back and forward and under and around, is to make double-dog certain that they're right because there'a a lot at stake.

Sometimes it helps to look at the line not just from behind the ball but from the side as well. That way, you might spot a slight rise or fall in the green that you couldn't see from the other angle.

As for the way to play the stroke, putting's a very individual thing. Being comfortable is really more important than any rules about how to stand.

30

Looking for the undulations . . .

'Being comfortable,' says Tony, 'is really more important than any rules about how to stand.' And there is little doubt who looks the most comfortable here – or why he holed out and I missed!

The Second

par 5, 490 yards

TONY This hole's really long.

MIKE It looks desperately difficult.

TONY It is, mate.

MIKE I want to go down there, do I?

TONY Yes, in the gap there.

MIKE Well, tell me how I line up. You see, I can't tell when I'm pointing in the right direction.

TONY The quickest way to check yourself is to place the club on the ground touching the toes of your shoes. Now come to the back of the tee and see where the club is pointing. In your case it's miles to the left and you'd have no chance at all of hitting the ball down the middle.

So let's start again. First, choose a spot in the distance that's in the direction you want. Imagine a straight line between you and that point. Now stand so that your shoulders are square to the line. . . .

I address the ball in that position, keeping my hands closer together as Tony told me on the last hole.

TONY That's better, a lot better. Now just keep it smooth and make a swing.

36

Lining up

The club placed on the ground touching the toe of my shoe gave the secret away –
that I had been aiming in the wrong direction, 'miles to the left'.

Driving from the tee with an iron

A good example of how not to do it. Some of the faults
picked up by Tony are: bunched-up stance results in shoulder
hitting chin on the backswing; the whole of the right side is
too stiff; right leg almost straightened.

In contrast, Tony in a much more relaxed position.

This is what we laughingly call my follow-through. Tony says
'It has stopped somewhere. The shoulders have straightened
and the body is off balance all together.'

How it *should* look. Tony's club has followed through on a
line, the swing is completed and the body properly balanced.

I swing – which is to say I hit the ground and then half-hit the ball, which plops into the rough a hundred yards away to the right.

> TONY Now, you lunged at it, you see. You took the club back but you tried to hit the ball with your belly. You didn't allow the club to swing. You didn't swing it with your arms. In addition, in trying to hit the ball with your body, you moved off it going back, hence the reason you hit behind it like that.

Tony hits a long one into the trees on the right of the fairway. He might be in trouble and I'm tempted to take advantage by attempting a 'big' shot from my rather difficult lie.

> TONY Don't make the mistake of getting too brave or ambitious with your club selection. You've got a tight situation here and I would advise a six iron just to get the ball properly on to the fairway and give yourself a good opportunity if you can for your next shot.
>
> MIKE That's being cautious.
>
> TONY No, it's being sensible. There's a difference.

At last I hit a shot to be proud of, with an easy swing. I'm relaxing more now in Tony's company and that seems to help. Must remember to ask him about mental preparation. . . . We go in search of his ball.

> TONY Oh, here we are! Give me a sand wedge, Viv, I'm in the oggin. I'm in a shocking spot here. The only thing to do in a position like this is to try to make sure I get the damn thing out, one way or t'other. It would be silly to try hitting towards the green because of all the trees in the way, so I'm just going to aim sideways, towards the fairway.

He does just that.

> MIKE Oh, great. But I was surprised at the way you played that shot because you seemed to jab at it.
>
> TONY Well I took a long backswing there and I hit down into

it as hard as I could because that grass is tough. I did 'stop' on it, but I brought the club very firmly into the back of the ball.

MIKE So it doesn't matter there if you don't follow through?

TONY Not in that situation. The main object there is to get the club in behind the ball and meet the ball first.

I take a five wood but don't connect too well. The ball goes straight but not very far – because I moved my head and lunged at the ball, says Tony. In contrast, his wood shot goes a very long way – but in the wrong direction.

TONY Oh, I've done it again. I keep hitting straight to the right this morning. I must have lined it up wrong. Now there's a lesson to be learned from my last shots and it's something that most club golfers don't take the time to consider in a situation like this. Remember, I hit my first tee shot to the right. My second tee shot went to the right. That shot there, with a four wood, went right. But I hit them all solidly. So from that one must deduce that technically I'm all right. It's my stance that's wrong.

I don't panic into thinking that my hands may be wrong at the top of my swing or that any number of other technical faults may be to blame. It's something more simple than that, more basic. It's my alignment. Far too many club golfers, when they hit a shot off line, start experimenting with grip, backswing and goodness knows what else and they never really establish a basis from which to work. Often the problem is very much more simple than they realize.

MIKE Right, how far is my shot to the green?

TONY 140 yards.

MIKE You know the course, but how would I assess the distance as a stranger to it?

TONY I simply know because I could get there with an eight iron. It might be 145 yards.

MIKE And you could get there with an eight iron! That's a five wood for me, I suppose.

43

TONY Well, a five wood like you hit on that first hole would put you past the pin.

MIKE So I should take a bit less than that, perhaps?

TONY But you told me earlier that you can't use the long irons.

MIKE Well, I'll have a go.

TONY Go on, then, with a four iron.

MIKE I want to do the right thing if I can.

TONY Of course, you want to play with the right club.

MIKE Am I lined up right?

TONY OK, you're lined up well. Just swing it. Don't hit it with your body now. Use your arms.

MIKE I hooked that badly and it didn't go very far, either.

TONY No, but you see you were too quick from the top of the swing. You never gave yourself time behind the ball to line up the club. You addressed the ball with the club slightly hooded in the first place.

MIKE What does hooded mean?

TONY It means the toe of the club was angled in towards your body. Hence the reason it was going in that direction. But the main fault was being too quick in starting down. You started to come down before you really got back. You never set the club at the top of the backswing, and then you sort of lunged at the ball. Again, you pulled your body in first. Hitting with your belly all the time!

  Say to yourself, 'I hooked it, so I must have swung from inside to outside.' Imagine a line between you and the hole; now we agree your body was lined up correctly, so to hit a hook – as you did then – you must have swung from inside that line to outside that line. You can't hit a hook any other way. It puts a spin on the ball that makes it go to the left. That's the one thing that you know you did.

  It's not possible to hook a ball and swing on a straight line. Nor is it possible to hook a ball by going outside and across the line.

It's inside to out that makes a hook. Once you know you've done that, you guard against doing it the next time. Similarly, what causes a sliced shot is to swing the club from outside the line to inside it. You have to know these basic things before you can start hoping to correct your faults.

Tony's shot reaches the green. I've landed on a downward slope.

TONY Now then, don't try to be clever in a situation like this. For the best player in the world it would be a difficult one, so I suggest you take a nine iron. It's a sandy lie, so you want to take the ball first. If you hit just behind the ball, you'll duff it, with the sand in between the face of the club and the ball. You don't have to hit far. You can stand with your legs together if you feel easier that way.

My shot is 'executed properly', according to Tony, but I hit it a little too hard and leave myself a long putt, which I fail to hole. Tony's putt goes down and I'm two down after two holes, a position that is all too familiar to me.

The Third

par 3, 130 yards

Tony takes a nine iron and lands on the green.

MIKE Not quite a hole in one. Now if you take a nine iron, what should I take?

TONY A six should be about right for you.

MIKE You think I should place it on a tee peg, do you?

TONY Of course you should. Every time you have the opportunity to tee it up, tee it up. If I do it, I'm sure that you should.

MIKE Right, am I facing in the right direction?

TONY Yes, you're all right. Try to get the ball a bit more forward. You see, if the ball's back, you have to stay back to hit it and you don't want to stay back. In all games you move forwards. In tennis you follow through, move forwards. Kick a ball – you move forwards. Punch – and you move forwards. Golf's the same. You move forwards after you've hit it.

MIKE And that's true of whatever club I'm using?

TONY Whatever club, yes... Now you've got yourself established in a comfortable position, swing the club. Forget everything else. Just swing the club, and I mean swing it.

48

I do what he says and I'm on the green!

TONY Look at that!

MIKE Good lord, I don't believe it.

TONY For a small fee, I'll accompany you on the world circuit if you like.

MIKE I'm thinking of turning pro now.

TONY Just before you think you've completely mastered the game, I must say that although you're making a better effort to swing the club, you get locked up in the backswing somehow. You don't swing enough behind the ball. You're a bit stiff and you don't swing as far back as you could.

MIKE Well, how far back should I go?

TONY Your body gets in your way when you're taking the club back. When I swing, my arms are independent from my body, do you see? If your arms don't move away from your body, how can you get your hands high? Try to allow the club (that's to say, your arms) to move away from your body a little bit on your back swing, especially your left arm. Yours is tucked so close into your chest that you're not allowing the club to get very high. In a subconscious effort to make up for that you give it the belly-shot.

I wish he'd stop talking about my belly.

MIKE This may seem a silly question after all you've said already, but what *is* a swing, anyway?

TONY A swing is ... well, the only reason you move any part of the anatomy at all is to allow the club to swing in a nice arc, in as smooth an arc as possible. The objective of golf as I see it is to make a smooth swing and the objective of anybody practising golf is to make the same swing every time, an action that you can repeat without question. I would say a swing is a free movement of the club without any impediments in it. The club should be allowed to take a smooth arc back on a line and the same smooth arc forward and through. That's what I always try to do.

49

The backswing

'Your body gets in your way when you're taking the club back. . . .

When I swing, my arms are independent of my body.'

I take two putts to record a three. So does Tony, but with my handicap shot I've won the hole!

> MIKE I'm going to tell the grandchildren about that – the day I beat Tony Jacklin on the third hole.

> TONY There's a very important mental lesson here. Golf is the greatest leveller of all times. If there's anything it teaches you, it's humility. As soon as you think you've got it beat, it'll come up and hit you right in the ... you know, hard!

All right, I'll try to be humble – but he's only one up after three holes and I can't help feeling I've nearly mastered the game.

The Fourth

par 4, 394 yards

TONY This is a dog-leg left – a blind tee shot – but all you need to do is hit it straight down the centre of this fairway, OK? The last red bungalow on the left up there is your line, so get yourself lined up for that. Swing the club through nice and smooth. I know I keep saying that until you're sick of hearing it, but it's the thing you've got to tell yourself over and over again.

I hit a straight one.

TONY Good man. That'll do you.

MIKE Not very far.

TONY A bit right – but what do you expect, miracles?

MIKE Yes.

Tony hits a corker straight down the middle.

MIKE Super shot! I was watching carefully there where you placed the ball in relation to your feet.

TONY Always in the same place. The old teaching was that with a driver you placed the ball opposite the left inside heel and pro-gressively moved it towards the right foot as the number of the club increased, until the wedge (or number ten) was opposite the inside of the right heel. In these modern days that practice has been completely changed so that the ball never moves off the left instep. Only the stance varies as the club gets shorter.

This happens quite naturally and automatically because a shorter (or higher-numbered) club comes closer to the body. You need the greater width of stance on a wood because it requires a bigger swing, and so you need it for extra balance. But the ball itself is always in line with the left instep or there-abouts – between the centre of stance and left instep.

We've walked to my ball which is in light rough. I take a five wood – and miss it completely.

MIKE An air shot! I see what you mean about humility. But how could I do that after all you've told me?

TONY Well, one of the dangers of telling you what you're doing wrong on every shot is that all I'm going to succeed in doing is to fill your head with a lot of mumbo jumbo. So rather than do that, I would prefer just to tell you to get comfortable again, and just think about swinging the club. Don't try to kill the ball. Don't try to knock the cover off it. There are no prizes for that. Swing it.

I strike the ball fairly well this time, though it lands in rough.

TONY You hit it very well but your main problem is still that you don't allow your arms to work independently. Nevertheless, if you worked at it and played a bit, I've no shadow of doubt in my mind that I could get you to single figures.

MIKE I find that hard to believe. Really?

TONY Oh yes, because you have an aptitude for it, I can see that, but you don't play often enough and you've had some bad basic advice from your friends.

Tony takes a nine iron and the ball describes one of those perfect arcs he was talking about to land on the green. It's the kind of moment when I wonder why I bother because that sort of excellence is surely unattainable by an amateur rabbit like me. Yet ten minutes ago I was thinking I'd

The line of the club

Tony explains the line between club head at point of impact
and left inside heel – whatever the club you are using.

'Only the stance varies as the club gets shorter,' he says, pointing out that this happens naturally as the shorter club comes closer to the body.

mastered the game! That's the old, old golfing story ... We walk on to find my ball in a horrible lie in scrub.

> TONY What do I tell you to do here? Pick it up! Seriously, if it were me, I would think that I could hit it hard enough with a wedge to get it out of that rubbish and over the hump in front, but I really can't see you doing that, so you're going to have to hit it sideways.

> MIKE Can't I try to do it your way?

> TONY Yes, certainly, have a go with a wedge, remembering again that the most important thing is to hit the ball first, because if you hit this grotty stuff behind it, you're going to slow the club down. Hit down into the ball as hard as you can.

It works. For once I do what he tells me and the ball sails out of the scrub and lands just short of the green.

> TONY Well done ... Another important thing to remember in golf is that everybody has a limit as to how hard or how far he can hit a golf ball. And it's very important to know your limitations. If you hit a nice ball by swinging (and usually not swinging hard) that limit may be attained. But subconsciously you think, 'If I hit it that far by swinging nice and easy, I can hit it a bit harder and it will go a bit further.' Not so. We all have a limit and I think the smart man finds his limit straight away and then he gets the urge to 'kill the ball' out of his system altogether.

I prepare to take my shot to the green.

> TONY Here you want to pitch the ball just short of the green and let it roll on. But you're standing as though you're trying to clout it a mile. You don't need to stand like that. This is a delicate shot here, not a damn great drive or anything like that. No need to stand miles away from it. You're making it more difficult than it actually is. Grip down the club; don't be afraid to compromise yourself a bit with your grip. Get close to the ball.

I play the ball well, Tony says, though too hard. It leaves me with a long putt which I fail to hole. He's down for three.

MIKE That's another win for you. My brief moment of glory over! Two down.

We walk towards the fifth tee.

MIKE I know a bad workman blames his tools, but would it make any difference to my game if I played with other balls? What difference does the size of the 'big' ball make?

TONY Literally point nought six of an inch in diameter. A bigger ball is more effective in a following wind because it's a larger mass. Smaller balls on the other hand tend to go through a head wind better. It's said that the big ball is just a bit easier to putt with because, being bigger, it's a bit easier to control on the greens. There've been arguments about that over the years, but the majority of world golfers now play with the big ball and in professional competition it's mandatory in most places. But I shouldn't worry your head about it, Mike. Your golf should improve, but I'm sure you don't expect to arrive at such a high standard that a fractional difference in the size of a ball is going to change your game.

The Fifth

par 3, 145 yards

Tony takes an eight iron and lands on the green.

MIKE I should take a five, should I?

TONY Five should be all right. Just take a practice swing first ...
Now you see you've never learned to turn properly. You're
all hunched up and when you look down at the ball and take
a swing, your shoulder's hitting your face. Mine goes under my
chin.

MIKE You've got a longer neck.

TONY No I haven't, you can't get away with that excuse! Try
again – and set yourself up properly.

MIKE Is that about right?

TONY Yes, but you're aiming left.

MIKE Is that better?

TONY Well, you've moved your stance to aim in the right direction, but your club is still aiming left. That's better. Now just
swing the club freely. Don't try to kill the ball. Swing the club
through the ball ...

Why can't I remember to do that – stop lifting my head? Here
Tony's iron is well through the ball and his head remains
down.

In a tricky situation like this, 'the aim must be to hit the ball
first, as opposed to the sand or stone'.

I hit my best shot of the day so far, though it's short of the green.

TONY That was a very good shot, even though you're a bit short.

MIKE I don't care if it's short if I hit it properly. That's a big thrill.

TONY But that's sad, really, because if we'd picked the right club for you, a three iron instead of a five, you'd have been up there on the green.

We walk to my ball which is lying on a stony, sandy path.

MIKE How on earth am I going to cope with that?

TONY Well, a lie like that isn't going to occur more than once in ten rounds. There's no right or wrong way to play it; you simply do the best you can. It's the right shot if it goes up near the pin! But however you choose to stand or to hold the club, the aim must still be to hit the ball first, as opposed to the sand (or a stone which would ruin your club). So hit down and through, ball first.

I scuff the ball only a few feet forward.

TONY You hit the sand first. But it was difficult, damned difficult for anybody, that, not just for you.

My next shot reaches the edge of the green. Tony holes his and I'm three down after five holes.

The Sixth

par 4, 320 yards

Between tee and green there's a huge hollow. Tony's drive flies over it, of course, though he's hooked it and is none too pleased with himself.

MIKE I really dread trying to drive across great chasms like this.

TONY You don't look at the chasm, do you? If you look down there, the tendency is that you're going to go down there. Instead, look at the point where you want the ball to finish.

MIKE You know what I mean, though, there's a kind of mental magnet about hazards in front of the tee.

TONY Of course – but it's not a mental magnet if you don't look at it. Look above it and say to yourself, 'Right, the first thing I must not do is to try to kill the ball to get it over there. I'm going to look on to the fairway, and I'm going to swing the club through the ball, not at it.' I promise you, if you hit through the ball like you did on that last tee, the thing'll fly out there nicely. Get yourself comfortable. Swing the club through the ball and don't try to murder it.

I do what he says and the ball sails over the chasm on to the fairway.

TONY You see, it's all in the mind, isn't it? You could stand here for five months and never hit a better shot than that.

Tony's drive on the 320 yard hole

Contrast in styles on the green.

There is little doubt which of us looks the better balanced,
'collected' and comfortable.

MIKE That's true. That went straight. That was quite exciting.

TONY Really, you can't expect to get better shots than that on a twenty-three handicap. If you could hit like that every time, you'd be twelve handicap or less wouldn't you, anyway? It's a question of convincing yourself of things, talking yourself into things. Just as you can talk yourself into missing a putt, you can talk yourself into holing one as well. That's what concentration's about. That's why you can't play golf and walk round talking and chatting. When you go out and play golf with someone who's at your level, if you want to improve, then you have to think what you're doing because it's a bloody difficult game. If you want to go out purely for exercise because you've got a fat belly or something like that, well then you may as well not have a ball there. You can walk a dog and do that.

I was saying earlier, by the way, that we all have our limitations. Now I'd say that shot of yours was just about the limit of your hitting. In the summer it would go another thirty yards further on a hard fairway and you'd finish with a drive of 210 yards or so, which you'd really be happy with. All I'm saying is that in a situation like this, you could stand on that tee and try to hit that ball, or a dozen balls, or fifty balls, harder and you wouldn't get any further than that. You've to get it into your mind that that is the best you can expect, and then try to achieve that consistently.

MIKE Right. Now my second shot is – what, 130 yards, do you reckon?

TONY Easily, 135 even. Hit a seven iron. It's uphill, you see, to the elevated green and that always means you should take at least one club bigger than for the same distance on the level ... You're aiming a bit left now ... That's better. Now don't get too excited about it; hit through it.

That's just what I do.

TONY Oh, what a great shot! I'm not saying any more, you've had it now! That's perched up there on the green beautifully.

Tony's second shot lands on the edge of the green and he's unhappy that it's 'a bit short'. However, he holes the long putt. Down in three. With my shot advantage I can beat him here, but my first putt is well short. My second putt, to halve the hole, misses too. I've thrown away my chance.

TONY What a shame.... Only you know this, so I'm going to ask you: When you were on the first putt there, did you really try to make it? Or did you think, 'Well, if I get it close...'

MIKE Oh no, I tried to make it. I promise you I did.

TONY Well, that's all right.

MIKE But I was rather lacking in guts, wasn't I?

TONY That's what made me think you were just trying to roll it up close. Pity to hit two marvellous shots like that and three-putt, isn't it? That's what makes the game so tantalizing. There you hit two career shots on to the green, but having come all this way in two shots, you take three more (which count just the same on the card) to go a few yards! Daft, isn't it? But you know, when you can hit the long balls consistently, this short game, the putting, is the area where you can really chop shots off.

The Seventh

par 4, 340 yards

Tony drives. 'A little bit left but it's all right.' I drive – my best yet. He seems to be getting through to me, making me feel that I really can improve and that I'm beginning to enjoy the game a lot more.

TONY Beautiful! Absolutely beautiful. I can't say more.

We walk up to my ball, which lies in a position from which I can't see the flag.

TONY I reckon you need a four iron here. And if you're going to miss it (and I'm not implying that you are) there's trouble on the right.

MIKE Well, I'm going to pretend I didn't hear you say that.

I hit a scorcher. This man's working miracles with me.

TONY That's absolutely perfect. It's really coming together. I think you've been having some secret sessions, mate!

MIKE Now the problem, as you warned me before, is not to get big-headed.

Tony takes his second shot, a glorious sand wedge that lands him on the green. That's where I thought I was, too, but as we approach it becomes

76

clear that I've dropped into the bunker beside the green. My turn for the sand wedge now. But I need help!

TONY I think that the first thing the majority of people do when they land in a bunker is panic! The average club player immediately starts worrying about whether he's going to get out or not. Yet it's one of the easiest shots to execute in the whole game of golf. Get the basic technique right and you should have no problems whatsoever.

The difference between a sand wedge and other irons like a pitching wedge or a nine iron is that whereas those irons will dig into the sand, a sand wedge has a bulge on the sole which gives the club the ability to 'bounce' on the surface of the sand. When I was a lad learning the game, my Dad used to talk about 'splashing' the ball out of the bunker and that's something I still aim to do, almost as though I am playing out of shallow water.

Open the blade and open the stance. Never hit at the ball, always through it. Never stop at it. When that feeling of panic I was talking about comes over you, the tendency is to take a hurried swipe at the ball with the result that the club digs deep into the sand instead of lifting the ball away. Instead, with that open stance and the club face nicely open, you should swing the club back freely and easily – though not for a long way – and 'splash' the ball out, always taking a little sand behind the ball.

We're talking now about greenside bunker play rather than long shots out of bunkers down the fairway. In that case, say 150 yards from the hole, the objective, if the lie was decent enough, would be to take the ball first and any sand afterwards on the follow-through. In a bunker like this, with fine sand, the simple 'splashing' shot that I've described will have two effects. It'll get the ball out of the bunker. And it will make the ball stop on the green instead of running through it, because the way the open club face meets the ball imparts the necessary backspin. However, if the ball is plugged deeply in wet sand, there's no possibility of your getting that backspin on the ball. There's going to be so much sand between the club face and the ball at impact that the ball must come out with overspin or no spin at all. There's nothing you can do about that!

MIKE But in these conditions which you seem to think are ideal

77

In the bunker

'One of the easiest shots to execute in the whole game of golf.'
Open the blade ...

... and open the stance.

(I'm trying not to panic, you see), how hard should I strike the ball?

TONY I wish you could get it into your head that the strength of so many shots – and certainly this one – around the green depends on what I've called 'feel'. Nothing else – no technical rules, no scientific measurement of force at impact or anything like that. As I said before, you feel the amount of strength needed in the same way as you feel how much muscle to use when you want to throw a ball a certain distance. But one thing you must never forget in this respect is that it's in the follow-through that you get this feeling. That's where the 'feel' is generated. You mustn't think of how hard you're going to hit from behind the ball; how hard you're going to hit *through* the ball is what matters.

MIKE One of the problems I find with bunkers is that they vary in texture so much. Some sand is hard and impacted like concrete. At other times it may be almost fluffy. How do you cope with these different conditions?

TONY By practising. That's the only possible answer. The texture of sand, like the texture of grass on the greens, may differ from week to week even on the same course, so there's really no alternative to practising and getting the feel of it. Around the world, of course, conditions vary dramatically. On some American courses, for instance, you can hardly call it sand, it's very fine grit. But then you could move on to another course in, say, Florida and find yourself playing off the beautiful white, packed sand there. The week after that you might be on a links course in England playing on fluffy dry sand. But essentially I would play the same shot in all those circumstances. The fundamental lesson to be learned about golf around the green, however, is that it cannot come right without constant practice. That is the only way to become a good chipper, good bunker player, good putter. It's my personal view that with long shots, once you've got that swing technique right, all you have to do is maintain it. But with the short game you must keep on practising on all the different lies that there are.

MIKE Back to my immediate problem in this bunker, do I still

stand with the ball opposite the inside of my left heel, as you
told me to do for all other shots?

TONY Yes, still the same, but with the stance a little more open
– in other words, the left foot back a bit more, aiming slightly
to the left of the hole.

I do what Tony tells me – and the ball does just what he said it would,
'splashing' out of the sand, landing on the green and stopping a few feet
from the pin as the backspin has its effect. We both sink our putts so,
with my shot advantage, that's a half. Only four down after seven holes
against a man who won the Open! I'm trying to be humble but I can't
help feeling elated.

The Eighth

par 3, 165 yards

Tony drives and drops on the green, as near to a hole in one as I've ever seen. I take a five wood and execute a shot that merely qualifies as 'not bad'.

TONY That was a case of 'making' the ball go there – you actually put it there as opposed to just swinging freely through it. Not a bad shot, though. You didn't do anything very wrong, so you just shrug your shoulders at that and you say, 'Well, I hit it nicely', and you don't get uptight about the fact that it wasn't better because we're talking about fractions of an inch if you think about it.

MIKE As we're talking about subtleties and while we're walking towards my ball, will you tell me something about etiquette? I'm never too sure, for instance, how to ask for a game with a professional. Let's say I arrive at a club in a strange town and there's nobody around and I want to ask the pro to play with me. What sort of arrangement should I make? Presumably I have to pay him to play.

TONY Yes of course, you go into the pro's shop and say, 'I'm a visitor to the area and I would very much like to play with the head professional, or if that's not possible, one of the assistants. I'd like to know if there's anybody available, and if so what their charges are.' Simple, just act as you would in any sports

Hitting out of the rough

As I prepare to hit out of the rough, Tony counsels against my 'shutting the face' of the club too much.

shop. If you were going into a ski shop to have a ski-ing lesson, you'd want to know what they charged per hour or whatever, wouldn't you?

MIKE And you'd pay a fee if you were just playing a round and not having a formal lesson?

TONY Yes – after all, you would hope that on the way round he would give you the odd tip. He wouldn't give you a lesson but if he saw you doing anything desperately badly he would try to straighten you out.

MIKE Now where am I?

TONY You're in the rough there to the right. I'd take a wedge in that position but perhaps you should try a nine iron. Pitch it on the edge of the green and let it run up to the pin. This time, don't shut the face so much.

MIKE What do you mean by shutting the face?

TONY Well, you have a tendency to have your hands ahead of the ball which brings the top of the club face too far forward. Let the club rest in its natural position on the ground: that's the proper angle at which the face should meet the ball. Now get yourself in as near the ball as you can so that you have more control.

I hit a messy shot and the ball scuttles through the long grass to land by the edge of the green.

TONY Again there you gave it that long back swing and then decelerated at the ball. The objective of golf nearly all the time is to be accelerating at the ball so I'd rather see you shortening that backswing a bit and concentrating more on the follow-through.

Tony requires two putts to hole out. I get down in two from the edge so it's another half. Sensational!

TONY I know one thing, Michael Barratt – you play more than three or four times a year, as you claim.

A messy shot with a nine iron. Tony says that I decelerated at
the point of striking the ball. 'The objective of golf nearly all
the time is to be accelerating at the ball, so I would rather see
you shortening the backswing a bit and concentrate more on
the follow-through.'

MIKE Not much more. I certainly haven't played more than a dozen rounds this year.

TONY But how often do you pop into a driving range?

MIKE Never. I don't like going to driving ranges because it always seems to me that golf is made up of so many different shots and if I just go and drive and drive and drive, it won't do me much good.

TONY That's very true, but any golf practice is better than none at all!

The Ninth

par 5, 485 yards

Tony drives and isn't pleased because he slices it. My own drive is actually straighter but a great deal shorter – just a yard or two short of a bunker, in fact. Tony recommends my five wood for my second shot.

MIKE It's in a difficult lie. Can I move it?

TONY Yes, it's on the fairway and winter rules are in operation. That means you can place it on a good lie. Always take advantage of the rule when you can. After all, it could be the difference between a cracking shot and a lousy one ... Now the green is still a very long way away so just aim straight for that white marker post ahead.

I put all my strength into a great lunge at the ball – and the club bites into the turf behind the ball, missing it completely.

TONY You tried to kill the ball, man. And that just won't work. The sooner you come to believe that the better.

MIKE I was too cocky again.

TONY That, too. It's a bit like Monopoly, this game. You think you're winning then suddenly it's off to jail and a £200 fine! The problem at this stage, after we've played nine holes, is to know what else to tell you – if anything at all, because if I'm not careful you'll just become totally confused and disheartened. And after all, how much better at the game do you really expect to get, if it's to remain a fairly infrequent hobby or even if you play every weekend.

You must know you'll never be able to go out and smash a ball 280 yards, so instead of getting bogged down in more technical jargon, just say to yourself, 'I hit six or eight shots today right off the button, straight down the middle, and they gave me a lot of pleasure. That's my Sunday best.' I think you should be happy with the way you've been playing today.

It's also difficult to know what to say to a beginner when he asks you, 'What am I doing wrong?' because he's probably doing at least ten things wrong. The best you can do in that case is to concentrate on one of the fundamental faults. In your case, I think you should be trying to get more flexibility into your swing. Look at the difference between your turn and mine. You're all stiff and ungainly and you look as though your left leg's a wooden one.

Stand with your legs naturally apart and your knees slightly bent. Now pretend that someone behind you calls your name. Turn naturally to look at him. That's the way your shoulders should move for the backswing. You'll notice at the same time that there's a certain resistance to that turn from the hips, which are in a position to draw the shoulders back to where they were. That's the position I'm in at the top of my swing – like a spring coiled up and ready to be released.

When my hips and big muscles – back and thighs – are in the right position, that spring coil is released – and there's nowhere my club can go but straight through.

My weight is maintained on the instep of my left foot throughout the swing. But your weight's all over the place as you straighten one leg and then the other and waggle your bottom all over the place.

You must never have anything straight in a golf swing, except maybe your left arm and that shouldn't be rigid. If it's straight, it's going to need a jerky movement to get it unstraight! So maintain a flexed position throughout.

However, as I say, there are dangers in confusing you by trying to correct too many errors. Let's play out this hole and then

The relaxed stance

On bended knee, Tony points out my own stiff-legged address position.

Well, he didn't actually beat me ...

take a rest from hitting the ball to sit down and think through
the principles of golf a little more carefully.

With some indifferent shots on my part, ending with a seven (net six)
and Tony getting a birdie, I'm five down and jump at the opportunity
to accompany Tony to his delightful home for a chat. I can always say
afterwards that Tony Jacklin didn't actually beat me....

The Home Half

MIKE When I started playing this game, from the very first day, I went out with a full set of clubs. Golfing friends told me that I was daft, especially using a driver, a number one wood, off the tees. They told me I should concentrate first on the irons and leave the woods alone until I was a better player. I didn't like that idea. I reckoned that I should try to play the proper clubs for the proper shots from the beginning. Right or wrong?

TONY I think you were probably more right than wrong. However, there are dangers. My own advice to anybody starting the game would be to say first that the longer the club you get in your hands, the greater the tendency for you to think, 'Gosh, it's a longer club so I must hit it a bit harder so that it will go a long way.' Even if it's only subconsciously, we all tend to think that if a ball is meant to travel further, we're meant to hit it harder. Of course, that's not the case at all.

Jack Nicklaus has said that one of the greatest pleasures he has had in his golfing career was when a film was made of his swing with a one iron, then another of his swing with a seven iron. The two pictures were superimposed and, to Jack's great delight, they showed that the speed of both swings was exactly the same. That is really the ultimate. That is what everybody must set out to achieve. The point is that it's the length of a club's shaft that dictates the distance the ball will fly, not the force with which you strike the ball.

So although I agree with your decision to play with the full range of clubs on the course, I suggest that when a beginner practises – and he has little chance of improving his game if he doesn't practise – he should do so with the medium irons, a five or a six, perhaps. That way, he knows he's not trying to hit the ball out of sight but is content to swing smoothly through the ball and see it travel 160 yards or so.

I often watch people practise. They start off with a few short irons and they can't wait to get to the driver. They tee up the ball and you can feel them thinking, 'Let me at it', as they slash around. They're wasting their time altogether because they're not making swings, they're making haphazard lunges at the ball.

I know there are many people who are content to hack their way around a course, cuffing the ball once perhaps 240 yards so that they can stand in the bar afterwards and brag: 'I hit the fifth hole with a drive and wedge', or something of the sort. Well, that's rubbish as far as I'm concerned. Let's try to play the game as it should be played otherwise it's no fun for the amateur – and starvation for the pro! The crucial thing, then, is to hit the woods consistently and straight. Do that with the proper timing and you'll have no problems about getting the distance. When using irons, and especially the medium and short irons, there's never any need to try to hit them flat out. For me, eighty-five per cent of my strength is all that's needed. That, you see, is the reason you have a set of different clubs. There's never any need to try to smash a seven iron, say, to the maximum of your strength because there's a six iron in your bag which will enable you to make the shot much more easily and smoothly to achieve the same distance but better accuracy.

MIKE We can't have every club, of course, because we're limited to fourteen in the bag. Should the number one wood be one of those for the amateur?

TONY Most certainly, in my view. Other clubs may have a variety of purposes and may be more or less suited to individual styles of play, but the driver is the one club that quite simply will produce maximum distance (provided you use it properly as I've just explained). You can experiment with different shafts – graphite and lightweight steel, whippy and stiff – or whatever

At Tony Jacklin's home, a contrast in styles that says
everything about the Dos and Don'ts of a golf swing ...

you like, but in the end the club that will give you an extra ten or twenty yards is the club for you.

MIKE Now how do you know, on the tee, that you have the face of that wood at the correct angle to the ball?

TONY You don't. It could be said that you only know whether you've got it right after you've hit the ball. We are, remember, dealing in minute fractions when we talk about the angle of a club face hitting a tiny spot on a tiny ball. Once you've got the grip right and your stance in the proper line, it comes down to what I call 'feeling' again. Instinct, if you prefer it. I'm a great believer in that.

MIKE But let me put it this way to you: if I rest the base of the wood on the ground behind the ball, is it at the right angle?

TONY Yes it is. But remember that you can so easily change that angle, perhaps without realizing it, by then gripping the club wrongly or setting yourself up in the wrong way. Some people worry about the effects of standing too far from or too close to the ball, which is yet another factor – but there's no complex technique involved here. If you ask exactly how far to stand away from the ball, the only answer is 'comfortable distance'. It's the point at which your arms are extended out in front so that you're not leaning or bending over; you're not putting the stress on any part of your body at all.

Look at any of the photographs of my stance while we were playing those nine holes earlier and you'll see that I'm in a relaxed position. Everything's well balanced and I'm comfortable. The last thing you want is to be trying to swing the club head through a 180-degree circle from an uncomfortable position. So, going back to your earlier question, the driver is important because it's the club that will get you distance when you want it. To a lesser degree that's true of the other woods.

MIKE But *which* other woods should I put in my bag? I have a one, a three and a five.

TONY That sounds like a good choice to me. You use your driver well and I think the majority of golfers find that three woods is the ideal number.

The angle of a club face hitting a tiny spot on a tiny ball . . .
'We are dealing in minute fractions.'

Setting yourself up in the right way . . .

... and the wrong way.
Tony stands at a comfortable distance from the ball with no stress on any part of the body. He is well balanced in every way. I am a bunched-up bundle of stress!

MIKE The five wood tends to be my favourite.

TONY I can understand that. It has a nice little loft on it and it gets you out of lots of difficult 'fluffy' lies. The only trouble with you is that you sometimes use it in light rough when you're trying to be too ambitious – trying to go for the green instead of doing the sensible, cautious and really competitive thing, as a Yorkshireman should, namely using a seven iron or something like that to be certain that you can get out of trouble. Still, a five wood is a very handy club indeed. It's the long irons that are the difficult ones for most club golfers to handle.

MIKE That's the one, two and three irons?

TONY The one iron really is a pro's club.

MIKE I was going to say I've never quite seen the point of having a one iron in the bag.

TONY I use a one iron for teeing off on narrow par four holes or in the summer on the British links courses for long shots which I know are going to run a long way. I can get as much distance out of that club in such conditions as I can from a wood – and more control. But as a general rule, longer irons are difficult clubs for the amateur to use because he sees that straight face down there in front of him at the end of a fairly long shaft and he gets an attack of nerves! He's probably seen a pro hit one of those long low balls that gradually rises up and finally comes down in a great arc to stop dead on the green. The picture inspires him – but puts the fear of death into him at the same time when he thinks about what can go wrong if he hits it badly.

Let's not kid ourselves, there's a chasm of a difference between the pro and the normal club golfer. If you start playing the game at the age of eight or ten and develop a good swing, plus a good grip, plus good club head speed, plus an aptitude for ball games ... then there's a chance that you'll be a good golfer. But if you take it up later in life for pleasure or for exercise, you have to come to terms with the fact that you're probably not going to become a world champion.

As for you, you'll get a helluva lot of pleasure out of the game if you are content to put together a few shots like some of those you hit out on the course with me today. You could certainly

get yourself down to about a twelve handicap if you didn't frit-
ter away shots around the greens; if you learnt a bit more about
technique; if you knew a bit more about what happens out of
different kinds of lie; if you didn't take too many liberties, and
if you didn't think you're a wee bit better than you are.

MIKE I promise you I'll be humble for evermore! You've given
me so much to think about that I'm going to ask you now to
give me three basic rules for playing better golf. That should
help me to extract the priorities from all the good advice.

TONY First of all, without any doubt, you need to develop a
good grip. That is absolutely basic. I've never yet seen a really
good player with a bad grip.

The sad thing about golf is that if you do one of the basic
things wrongly at the beginning, you stymie your progress for
ever. You simply never get any better. Thus, if you have a bad
grip you might with luck get down to a fourteen handicap –
but fourteen is where you will stay, chum. That's it.

You know, I go back occasionally to where it all began for
me – the club at Scunthorpe – and I still see fellows I played
with twenty-five years ago when I took up the game. They
were eighteen handicap then and they're eighteen handicap
now. They have certain fundamental faults and because they
won't change them, because they persist in 'doing it their way',
they'll never play good golf. Grip, as I say, is number one. A
good neutral position with both hands so that one hand isn't
fighting the other and taking the club away.

Number two, alignment. Assuming that you have started by
getting the absolute essential, the grip, right and have progressed
from there to develop a reasonable swing which is more or less
the same every time, then you would do well to spend a great
deal of time trying to perfect this. It sounds very simple, just
making sure that you're aiming in the right direction, but this
is one of the most common errors that club golfers make. They
think they're aiming straight and in fact they're aiming to the
right or the left. You did it yourself when we were out on the
course. Laying down the club on the ground in the line that
your feet were actually pointing was quite a shock to you,
wasn't it?

There's no point in painstakingly developing a regular swing

The three golden rules

Develop a good grip – 'a good neutral position with both hands so that one hand is not fighting the other and taking the club away'.

Alignment. 'Simply' making sure that you are aiming in the right direction.

Ball position. 'Opposite the inside of your left heel, or perhaps
a fraction nearer the centre of the stance. And that is where it
should be for every shot.'

if every time you hit the ball you're sending it the wrong way, is there?

Similarly, it's a waste of time to swing properly if the ball itself isn't where it ought to be. So that's my third golden rule – ball position. I've told you where to place the ball – opposite the inside of your left heel, or perhaps a fraction nearer the centre of the stance. And that's where it should be for every shot, from a drive to a short chip. Again, as with alignment, you think it's a simple matter and you think you're doing the same thing every time, but without noticing it you may gradually be putting that ball further backwards or forwards. So many golfers, when they find that their game is deteriorating for some unexplained reason, almost inevitably think that it must be something to do with the swing. What's happening at the top of the backswing? Are they getting their hips out of the way? These sort of questions come into their minds and they start all sorts of pointless experiments which, if anything, make matters worse. Even you, with your unorthodox hip movement (I'm trying to put it politely!) do more or less the same thing hole after hole. The thing that *does* change, however, without your realizing it, is the ball position. Put it another way: if the ball is six inches further forwards than your best position for it, you'll still make the same pass at it but you won't get to the ball properly because your normal swing won't reach it at the correct moment. So check where that ball is again and again and again.

MIKE I was going to suggest that you might have a fourth basic rule and that's the right mental attitude. But I'm not sure what that is. On the one hand I keep being told to relax, to loosen the muscles, not to be tense and so forth, but at the same time you tell me off if I chatter as we walk round the course and you demand that I concentrate very hard all the time. It puzzles me how I'm supposed to do both.

TONY The right mental attitude? Difficult to establish, I agree. It's a subtle blend and the only word I can think of to describe what you want to achieve is 'freedom'. We considered all sorts of technical questions on the course today, but I didn't want you to start getting uptight about them. I wanted you to feel as free as possible. Uninhibited. When you addressed the ball, I didn't want you to be worrying, 'My god, I've got to do this and that and the next thing.' You can't play golf like that. You can't erect too many fences. There are enough there already! Essentially what I was trying to instil in you today was the freedom to stand up and make a pass at it: 'Let's make a swing at it for a start, let's get the show on the road before we do too much talking . . .' So many people never get off the tee, do they? They stand there and they're so full of theories from a great pile of golf books they've read – and maybe a dozen pros who've given them lessons, not to mention their mates at the bar in the club-house.

MIKE But a beginner must start with a lesson from someone. How should he choose a teacher?

TONY In the simplest terms, by finding a pro who you reckon is a regular sort of fellow; it's no use walking into any pro's shop and saying, 'Make me into a golfer'. You have to know what type of individual you're approaching first and whether his outlook is the same as yours so that you will respect him as a person and listen more willingly to his advice. It's a bit like going to get your hair cut. I wouldn't go to any old barber. Not on your life! I've sat in barbers' shops and watched the fellow in front of me getting his hair cut and I've walked out, thinking, 'I'm not letting that chap loose on my scalp. He might be technically proficient with a pile of certificates from hairdressing academies, but he's not for me.'

At the end of the day, when the talking has to stop, when you've picked your pro and absorbed the basic essentials that we've been discussing, playing better golf is a matter of common sense. There's no fluke to playing good golf, I promise you. There's a plain and simple reason for everything that happens. And don't be bamboozled by all those theories and silly superstitions. You've heard them: 'I play well when I go out and get drunk the night before . . . or if I go to bed and sleep for ten hours before a round, I always play badly.' Nonsense! You have to play better if you get good rest and your mind's clear and you're able to assess things better.

As I say – common sense!

The Clubs

MIKE When I took up the game, I bought a second-hand set of clubs for £20, primarily because I couldn't afford to buy a new set then but also because it seemed silly to splash out a lot of money on clubs before I'd even learned to swing.

TONY That was the right idea – and if I know you, with your Yorkshire hardheadedness, you wouldn't lose much when you finally traded them in for a new set.

MIKE I sold them a year later for £30 actually, which helped to persuade me that golf wasn't such an expensive game as its critics like to make out! But cost apart, my problem when it came to buying a new set was that I had no idea what I was looking for. There I was in the pro's shop, surrounded by countless makes, and not knowing where to begin.

TONY Very difficult. It's an individual thing, this, and I'm inclined to say that it's what takes your fancy that's right for you. However, it's going to mean splashing out quite a lot of money for a full set and maybe a bag to hold them, so you want to be as sure as possible that you're going to be happy with them. I'd certainly recommend playing a round or at least a few holes with a set of the same kind as the ones you think you'll buy. Perhaps the pro will have a used set that he'll lend you, or knows of another club member whose clubs you might borrow.

There's a lot of fascination in the whole business of club design – especially since my American friend Karsten Solheim developed his revolutionary Ping putter, which led him and his sons on to designing a full set of woods and irons, and in turn influenced the thinking of most other club manufacturers in the world. If you ever get a chance to visit the Solheims in Phoenix, Arizona, take it: you'd learn a lot about the fundamentals of club design that might even help your game!

By one of those strokes of luck that can only be called uncanny, I found myself a few weeks later on a trip to Western America and decided to stop off at Phoenix to visit the Ping factory. There I talked to Allan Solheim about first principles.

MIKE What really matters about the design of a club for a second-rate amateur like me?

ALLAN Well, if you want to improve your play, I do feel it is very important that you're 'fitted' properly. Some people are tall, some short and it's very important that, for instance, the lie of the club is right for each individual.

MIKE What do you mean by the 'lie' of the club?

ALLAN Whether the toe is up or down. In other words, the sole should generally be parallel with the ground for the ball to go straight. If the toe is up in the air, then the ball will hook or will be pulled left. If the toe is down, a player will push it right and fade the ball.

MIKE So the ordinary golfer would begin by checking that when he's in the address position, the sole of the club head is absolutely level ... What do you look for next?

ALLAN I think the next thing is the length of the shaft and the size of the grip. The length of the shaft is determined by the player's height and his finger-tip distance to the ground. This also helps to determine the lie of the club; if the fingers are closer to the ground, use a flatter club. You might think that a tall person would need a longer club, but that wouldn't necessarily be so if he had long arms!

123

Allan gave Mike this diagrammatic representation of club lies.

The heel is too high and a more upright club lie is needed to fit this golfer's height and stance.

This is the correct club lie for this golfer's height and stance.

The toe is too high. This golfer needs a flatter club lie for his height and stance.

MIKE What's the average distance from finger-tip to ground? Can you give some examples?

ALLAN Well, twenty-eight inches is standard and it varies from about twenty-five inches up to – well, we had someone in here who was thirty-one inches.

MIKE So, with a standard twenty-eight-inch distance from finger-tip to the ground, what then should be the length of the shaft of the club?

ALLAN It should be standard length, which is thirty-nine and a quarter inches.

MIKE And the thickness of the grip?

ALLAN That depends on what size glove you wear, or – to put it another way – what size hand you have. As a rough guide, if you wear a medium or medium-large glove, you would need a standard size grip. A large glove might mean a thirty-second of an inch over size, or extra large a sixteenth of an inch over size. A small glove would mean a thirty-second of an inch under size.

MIKE So with my small fat hands...

ALLAN I would say yours would be a thirty-second under size.

MIKE If you wanted to be more precise, how would you measure the hands?

ALLAN We measure from the beginning of the hand to the end of the finger-tips – which for most people will be about six and a half inches.

MIKE But is it normally possible for the ordinary customer in a little club shop to specify different sizes of shafts and grips to suit his individual requirements?

ALLAN I think so, at least with some manufacturers. As far as we're concerned here, every order's a special one. We build no standard stock at all. Every club that we produce is made up to an individual specification on order.

MIKE Now what about balance? When I talk about 'balance' in

most other things, I'm talking usually about the centre of gravity – finding a point where the thing is easy to pick up, if you like, because the weight on each side of that point is equal. But I don't see how that can apply to golf clubs. After all, we grip them at the top of the shaft, not halfway down.

ALLAN It's the weighting of the club head that we're really concerned about. The conventional thinking for many years was to outweight directly in the centre – to get the weight behind the ball, as they say. But this led to a tendency for the club head to turn. Look at a skater to get an idea of the principle. If he holds himself in close, it's easier for him to spin. If he puts the weight out, by putting his arms out, it's harder for him to turn. This was my father's idea to begin with – that the weight should be further out. So he started to drill holes in the centre of the club heads and so spread the weight. That's the basis of our design and increasingly, it seems, of others.

MIKE But Ping apart, how can someone like me pick up, let's say, a five iron in a shop and say, 'That's nicely balanced'? If I said that, I wouldn't really know what I was talking about!

ALLAN I think you can *feel* the balance in it. I think we all have something in us that makes us sensitive to this.

MIKE Do you vary the shape of the club face?

ALLAN Yes. On woods, for instance, with someone who can't stop fading the ball, we can close the face (make the face point left of the target) so that he'll hit the ball straight. Most of the touring professionals we've found use from about square to about one degree closed on the face of a wood. Very few of them use open face.

MIKE It's comforting to hear that pros can have problems, just like the rest of us!

ALLAN Whether they're really 'problems' would be difficult to say, but it does seem from their experience that the club face that is square to one degree closed is the one that performs the best.

MIKE But you know what they say, that a bad workman blames his tools ... Is it really the right thing to do, to select, say, a club face that's closed if you have a fade problem, rather than trying to cure what's wrong with your swing, or with the three essentials that Tony has told me about – grip, alignment and ball position?

ALLAN Oh, I think you definitely need to cure what's wrong with your swing! But the way I look at clubs is the same way as a carpenter cares about keeping his tools sharp. If he cuts wood all the time and never sharpens his saw, that saw's going to get dull and, in golfing terms, his game's going to get bad. If he sharpens it, he's able to cut through the wood much better and his game's improving!

MIKE What about irons?

ALLAN In irons we cannot change the 'open and closed' angles because they're more of a blade face. With irons, what we're concerned about is whether the toe is up or down, determining the lie of the club.

MIKE And the heel? I notice some clubs have rounded heels which won't touch the ground when the club head goes through.

ALLAN Yes, we ourselves have both the heel and the toe taken up so that a player is more likely to hit the centre of the club head and not throw the face open or closed.

MIKE I can have fourteen clubs in my bag, one of which is a putter. Which other clubs ought I to have?

ALLAN I think most good players will use a one, three and four in the woods, then a two to nine, pitching wedge and sand wedge in irons. However, I think it depends a lot on the course you're playing. If you're on a course where you want a wood to get distance plus a little height on it, you might put a five wood in the bag rather than a four.

MIKE Now the putter. That seems to be an almost impossible choice.

ALLAN Well, we thought we'd made just about the perfect putter – but we then had to make forty-nine others! People have immensely varied tastes with this club. As Tony must have told you, it's more a question of *feel* than anything else.

127

MIKE Some putters have a sort of kink in the shaft before it goes into the blade. What's that all about?

ALLAN I think the main reason for that is that you want your hands in front of the face. If the hands are leading, then they tend to pull it straight. It's like pulling a wagon; you can pull it straight but if you push it, the chances are that it will go off crooked. The same way with a putter; the hands should be in front.

MIKE Going back to the big clubs, a number of my more boastful golfing friends tell me they can get more distance by using expensive graphite shafts. Are these clubs worth the money?

ALLAN That's almost impossible to answer. I had a graphite club that just didn't seem to perform for me at all. My brother picked it up one day and started using it regularly because he found he was hitting the ball with it so much further than he was hitting with his standard driver. Later, I was approached by one of our customers who was having problems with his graphite driver. Said he didn't get distance and so forth, so I went out and tried it. I hit with it better than I've ever hit with anything! I used it for about six months and gave him his money back and was very glad to. So you see, there are no definite rules about types of club.

MIKE Finally, when the decision is made and I've bought the clubs, how do I look after them? Let's take the woods first.

ALLAN The last coat that goes on the woods when they're made is polyurethane, which pretty well moisture-seals the clubs. If you're in a very humid climate, you might want to wax the clubs once a month or so, to keep them moisture-sealed, but the polyurethane seems to stand up very well. Just wiping with a cloth is about all you need to do with woods.

MIKE But should you keep gloves on them to protect them in the bag?

ALLAN Yes definitely, because otherwise pulling out your irons will dent the wood.

MIKE And how should I look after the irons?

ALLAN Quite easy. Wipe them clean when you need to. You don't have to use soap or anything like that. Just water and a rag occasionally will keep the clubs clean.

The Last

Back from America, I plunged into the Pro-Am season at home, armed with a new set of clubs and – more important – a new confidence in my abilities, stemming from the Jacklin tutelage. This was to be my year, when I'd cover the piano top at home with trophies from countless courses nationwide.

The first public appearance of the new me was, however, a disaster. I managed to drive off the first first tee a hundred yards or so without decapitating any spectators – but my first attempt at a shot with a five wood on the fairway put a smile on the face of the ball and wiped it off my own. Successive 'top shots', air shots, slices and hooks quickly persuaded our band of followers to forsake us and join up with other personalities whose golf, unlike mine, was worth watching.

'You're not taking the club back far enough,' said my professional partner.

'You're coming off the ball on the downswing,' said the amateur making up our threesome. What on earth did he mean by that?

For the rest of the round, as the quality of my golf declined even further, I was bombarded with advice.

At the end of the day, deflated like a pricked balloon, I left for home believing that all Tony's instruction had been a waste of time, which, of course, was a stupid thing to think. Further reflection made me realize that I'd foolishly broken just about every rule he had laid down for me during that round in Jersey.

For a start, I hadn't been as fit as I might have been. And as Tony Jacklin had pointed out, it's nonsense to think that you can play your best golf on too little sleep and too much high living.

Then, I had allowed all that advice from my friends to throw me into a state of confusion and eventual panic. How silly to forget the three golden rules: grip; alignment; ball position. I resolved to keep repeating them mentally throughout the next match, to the exclusion of everything else.

And that is how, in a star-studded field at the Variety Club's Cel-Am in Guernsey a week later, I at last learned my lesson the Jacklin way. 'You're a bandit,' someone in the gallery shouted as I picked the ball out of the hole to record my third gross par in succession – that's to say, three net birdies taking into account my twenty-three handicap. No one has ever been so thrilled to be accused of being a bandit!

Grip. Alignment. Ball position.

For eighteen holes I recited the magic words and the effect was so marked that not only did our team amass forty-three Stableford points but I *enjoyed* the golf in a way that Tony said I should.

There were many bad moments in the round, of course. But almost every one was due to my concentration on the basic rules lapsing for a moment, or to my forgetting other simple tips Tony had given me. For instance, on one hole, with the ball sitting on one of those nasty uphill slopes, I omitted to compensate for the natural tendency to hook the ball – and it sailed away to the left into a gorse bush. That time, or to be honest, time and time again, a blob on the card was quite unnecessary. If only I'd done what he'd told me ...

I suppose all our rounds of golf will forever be sprinkled with 'if onlys', but I also know that rabbits like me could play much better golf than we do by paying attention not to the subtle and complex advice of the armchair experts but to words like these:

'Feel as free as possible. Uninhibited ... At the end of the day, when the talking has to stop, when you've absorbed the basic essentials that we've been discussing, playing better golf is a matter of common sense.'

Yes, Tony, I believe you!

Index